LIVING IN
SPACE
By Felicity Trotman

CONTENTS

SKYLAB

Skylab was the only American space station. Just 63 seconds after launch, a shield designed to protect it from meteroids came loose and jammed one of the solar panels. *Skylab's* protection from the Sun's heat was lost, and the temperature inside went up to 52°C (126°F). The astronauts' first task was to cool it down. In total, three crews, of three astronauts each, worked on *Skylab*. They studied Earth's resources, the physics of the Sun, and human medicine. *Skylab* fell back to Earth in July 1979.

SPACE TIME LINE

DID YOU KNOW?

• In 1961... Yuri Gagarin was the first man in space.

• In 1969... Apollo 11 was launched and Neil Armstrong was the first man on the Moon.

• In 1971... the Soviet Union's Salyut 1 was the first space station to be launched.

• In 1973... Skylab was launched by the USA.

• In 1979... Skylab fell back to Earth.

• In 1981... the first orbiting space shuttle was launched (Columbia).

• In 1986... the first part of the Russian space station Mir was placed in orbit.

• In 1998... the Russians announced Mir to be decommissioned, and the first module of the ISS was launched into space.

WHAT SPACE STATIONS ARE

For hundreds of years, humans have dreamed of travelling in space. We want to explore the Moon and the planets, and venture out beyond the Sun. Space stations are an important step towards achieving this goal. They are giant satellites which are carried into space in pieces, called modules, and joined together in orbit. Large enough for people to live in, these stations are used as laboratories and observatories. They allow longer and more complicated experiments to be carried out and provide important information about the effects on humans of living in space. This research is essential if manned flights into space are to continue. It also brings us benefits back on Earth – items such as laptop computers, trainers and even crisp packets are all a result of space technology. The first space station was *Salyut 1*, launched by the Soviet Union in 1971. Now a new space station, the *International Space Station (ISS)*, is being constructed by 16 countries, led by the USA. It is the biggest and most complicated space project ever.

SATURN V

The *Saturn V* rocket was built to carry men to the Moon. It was the biggest rocket ever made. After the *Apollo* missions to the Moon finished, the USA's National Aeronautics and Space Administration (NASA) decided to use part of a remaining *Saturn* rocket to build an orbiting space station. The result was *Skylab*, built using a huge spare fuel tank from the rocket. The space station was 36 metres (118 ft) long and 6.4 metres (21 ft) in diameter, the size of a small three-bedroomed house. It was launched on 14 May 1973, the last time a *Saturn V* rocket was used.

APOLLO-SOYUZ

In 1973, the Soviet Union and the USA started to work together on some space programmes. This included the meeting in space of two crafts, *Soyuz* and *Apollo*, launched on 15 July 1975. Above you can see *Apollo* on the left, and *Soyuz* on the right.

MIR

In 1986, the Soviet Union launched the first modules of a new space station, *Mir* (meaning peace). It was designed to grow into a big complex, with six docking ports and many modules added on. In its final configuration, *Mir* had grown to five times its original size. The last module, *Priroda* (nature), was added in 1996.

THE SALYUT STATIONS

After *Salyut 1* was launched in 1971, the Soviet Union launched six more *Salyut* space stations. Experiments included studying the effects on humans of staying in space for long periods of time. *Salyut 7* was launched in May 1982. It was used until the arrival of *Mir* in 1986.

SPACELAB

Spacelab was built by the European Space Agency (ESA), and first launched from the USA in December 1983. It was carried in the space shuttle's cargo bay, which is about the size of a railway freight wagon. A small tunnel joined it to the shuttle's flight deck. *Spacelab* was a space laboratory on which many European astronauts worked. It measured 4 metres (13 ft) in diameter and weighed about 11,350 kg (25,022 lb). It could be used for up to a fortnight – the time the shuttle could stay in orbit.

ZARYA

In 1999, *Zarya* and *Unity*, the first two modules for the new *International Space Station*, were joined together. *Zarya* (sunrise), a cargo module, was launched by Proton rocket in 1998. It's more than 12.5 metres (43 ft) long and 4 metres (13 ft) in diameter, and weighs about 24 tonnes (2,000lb). Although built and launched in Russia, it was paid for by the USA.

FREEDOM

After *Skylab* fell to Earth, the USA had no space station. This picture shows *Freedom,* a new station which the USA began planning in 1984. Building was delayed, and costs soared. *Freedom* was redesigned as *Alpha*, but this was still too expensive. The station was redesigned again, and other countries were invited to join in. The new station became the *International Space Station*.

VENTURE STAR

A new launch vehicle is needed to take the place of the ageing shuttle. The new system must be reusable and as economical as possible. This half-size *Venture Star* is being tested as one possibility. It is designed to cut launching costs by 10% and is completely reusable. It has a new kind of rocket engine, called a linear aerospike, which can adapt itself to changing atmospheric pressure. The vehicle's surface is covered with metallic tiles designed for a slower, cooler re-entry into Earth's atmosphere.

THE SHUTTLE AT WORK

The space shuttle will be used to carry modules, equipment and crews to the *ISS* at least until 2012, and possibly until 2020. Of the four shuttles, *Atlantis, Discovery* and *Endeavour* will do most of the work, because *Columbia* cannot carry heavy payloads. But the shuttle is expensive to launch and is also growing old – it first flew in 1981.

DOCKING

Docking is a highly critical part of reaching a space station. The transport vehicle has to match its speed with that of the orbiting station. At the same time, it must align its docking port with that of the space station. The two ports can then be brought together. The pilot has to manoeuvre carefully to avoid damaging the space station or his own craft.

THE DANGEROUS LAUNCH

Astronauts are issued with special clothes for their mission. They wear partially pressurized space suits for launching and re-entry to Earth. These are designed to protect them in case of accidents. Launching is especially dangerous. There is enough fuel in the shuttle's tanks to explode with the force of a small nuclear bomb, and there is no way to escape once it has been ignited.

GETTING THERE

Reaching a space station is not easy. Astronauts have to use the thrust of a rocket to overcome the gravitational pull that holds everything onto Earth's surface. The rocket engine carries them through the layers of gas in Earth's atmosphere to around 300-400 km (190-250 miles) above, where the space station is positioned in a low-Earth orbit. The astronauts must then dock, which is no simple task when the station is travelling at 27,000 km/h (16,700 mph)! Only when the transporter and the space station are very securely joined together can the astronauts move from one to the other. The first astronauts to visit the *International Space Station* will fly on the **Space Transportation System**, better known by its nickname, the space shuttle.

WE'RE OFF!

Packing for a trip is quite straightforward for most people, but going into space needs precision packing! There is a limited amount of room in the space transporter and in the space station. The weight of everything must be carefully calculated. As well as astronauts, the transporter carries equipment such as food, clothes, mail, tools, new material for experiments and replacements for any worn-out parts.

SPACE ACTIVITY

TRAVELLING IN SPACE

Going into space is expensive! At present, it costs about $20,000 (£13,000) to deliver one kilo (2 lb) to low-Earth orbit by rocket.

Imagine that you're going on a mission to the space station. Pack a bag with what you will need for a fortnight's stay. Remember, you can't get to the shops if you've forgotten anything!

Weigh your packed bag. What would it cost to deliver that number of kilos/pounds to the space station?

Weigh yourself. What would it cost to deliver you there?

AIRLOCK

An airlock is used to ensure that astronauts can move from one atmospheric pressure to another without getting 'the bends' – bubbles of gas in their blood which could be fatal. It's important that the atmosphere of the transporter vehicle and the space station is kept under pressure at all times. If either lost pressure, the astronauts' blood would boil!

BEDROOM & BATHROOM

There is no day or night on a space station, but it is usual to keep to Earth times. The *International Space Station* will work a 24-hour day. That means that at any one moment, shifts of astronauts will be working, relaxing, and sleeping. Normally, an astronaut gets eight hours each day for sleep. For cosmonauts to sleep in, *Mir* had two small cabins, the size of phone boxes. Each cabin had a sleeping bag attached to the wall, a desk that folded down from the wall and a porthole. Crews visiting for a short time slept in the living quarters, while cosmonauts used sleeping bags tethered to the ceiling! Cosmonauts normally had nine hours they could use for sleeping. Even so, some found that after many months in space, they had trouble sleeping, and felt exhausted. Another problem is that there is no water in space. All water is flown up to the space station with other supplies. It has to be carefully used – on *Mir*, it was rationed.

TAKING A SHOWER

Astronauts on the *ISS* can enjoy a proper shower. The shower will be sealed, so that not a drop of water escapes. Used water will be carefully collected, cleaned, and recycled. *Skylab* was the first space station to have a shower. It was collapsible, and could be used once a week, but it leaked! The drops had to be caught, in case any of them got into the electrical system and caused a short circuit.

USING THE LOO

On Earth, gravity causes body waste to fall away through a pipe. Waste from this space loo is sucked down a funnel by air, moved by a fan. The water is extracted, cleaned and recycled. The remaining urine is released into space. Solid waste is collected in bags. These are either packed into an unmanned cargo craft, which burns up as it falls to Earth, or returned to Earth and disposed of there. *Skylab* was the first space station to include a loo, and astronauts used seat belts to hold themselves in place!

SPACE STATION BEDROOM

The *ISS* has personal sleeping quarters for up to seven crew members. Each cubicle (see above) has storage space, a worktable, a computer terminal and a sleeping bag. It's also possible to use special blankets and sheets which have weightlessness restraints. This is a huge improvement from conditions in the early days of living in space. The first astronauts slept in their seats, or used hammocks which could be taken down and stored when not in use.

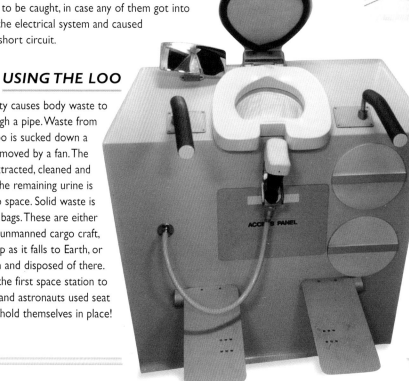

SPACE ACTIVITY

SLEEPING SCIENTISTS

There is enough room on a space station for 16 astronauts to sleep, and there are nine screens to divide the space up. The captain puts people who speak the same language together. On a previous mission, eight astronauts spoke English, five spoke Russian, two spoke Spanish, and one spoke French. The sleeping area was arranged like this:

A new crew of 16 astronauts is arriving; six speak Chinese, six speak Arabic, and four speak Swahili.

How can the captain rearrange the sleeping area for them by moving just two screens? Remember, he must keep together those astronauts speaking the same language.

(You will find the answer on page 30.)

HAIR CUTTING

Hair grows in space! Some astronauts have grown beards to avoid shaving. On *Skylab*, the shaving mirror was made of metal, as glass might have broken, which would have been very dangerous. The crews couldn't see their faces properly when they shaved, and they cut each other's hair. A small vacuum cleaner was used to suck up the clippings, otherwise, with no gravity to make them fall to the floor, they would float in the air. Astronauts could breathe them in and choke if they were not removed.

ASLEEP IN SPACE

In free fall, it's possible to sleep anywhere. In the space stations before the *ISS*, for comfort and safety, sleep restraint bags were fastened to the wall if there were no bunks. Scientists working in *Spacelab* slept in the shuttle, using the bunks or wall space.

GETTING CLEAN

Wet wipes have been used for many years in space. They are useful for cleaning the spacecraft, as well as the astronauts! Most early cosmonauts kept clean by using them. Shuttle astronauts decided not to bother with a shower – they preferred wet wipes.

A BED ON SKYLAB

Skylab was big enough to allow crew members separate sleeping quarters. Their work schedule allowed them between six and eight hours sleep a night. The astronauts, like Alan Bean (below), were strapped into their bunks so that they didn't float about.

PLAYTIME

Astronauts on *Discovery* conducted experiments with 11 toys – 10 that were launched with them (including this clockwork mouse), and a paper aeroplane they made while in orbit. With no gravity, the toys did not behave as they do on Earth. The jacks floated in the air and the ball was bounced off the shuttle wall. Other toys in space included a basket of stuffed animals. They were sent to Shannon Lucid on *Mir* by her children.

BOOKS IN SPACE

Books are a perfect way for an astronaut to relax, especially if they are read in bed! When Shannon Lucid spent six months on *Mir*, she read 50 books. They were strapped into a zero-gravity bookcase.

GETTING OUT OF UNIFORM

Astronauts are issued with the clothes they will need for their mission. These astronauts on the shuttle *Discovery* also took holiday clothes. Laundry is a problem in space as there isn't enough water to wash clothes. This means astronauts may have to go on wearing dirty clothes. On *Mir*, cosmonauts could only change their underwear once a week. Dirty clothes are bagged up and brought back to Earth to wash. Paper underwear can be disposed of with other rubbish. The Russians are trying to develop a kind of bacteria that will eat dirty underwear!

LIVING QUARTERS

Space stations can be noisy, smelly places. Machines that pump and clean air and water run all the time but cooking and bathroom smells can linger. Another problem is that there is no 'up' or 'down' in space. *Skylab* had no artificial directions built in, but the *ISS* copies *Mir* in having 'ceilings' with strip lights and 'floors' with dark panels. The tops and bottoms of hatches and airlocks are marked and there is a bright colour scheme. The *ISS* will have more space to live in – there may be up to 16 astronauts on board when crews change over. Crews may spend months on a space station, keeping in touch with their families by e-mail and post brought on the supply craft.

SMOOTH SURFACES

Early space stations had very cluttered living quarters. Boxes of equipment and experiments were scattered over all the surfaces. The *ISS* will be different. There will be smooth surfaces, with equipment tidied away behind access panels. A habitation module will make a permanent living space for the crews. It will measure 8.5 metres (28 ft) long and 4.25 metres (14 ft) in diameter.

MIR

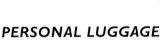

The living space on *Mir* was a long, thin room. It was rather like living in a railway carriage. Although there is no 'up' or 'down' in space, psychologists said it would be better for cosmonauts if *Mir* showed these directions. So the 'floor' had a carpet, the 'walls' were painted dark green, and the 'ceiling' was white.

PERSONAL LUGGAGE

It is possible for astronauts to take small personal items into space. Alan Shepard took a golf club to the Moon on *Apollo 14*. British cosmonaut Helen Sharman took a brooch to *Mir*. American astronauts each have a Personal Flight Kit, or PFK. They must account for every item in it, to be sure there is nothing too big or too heavy. One of the most popular activities is watching and photographing Earth from the windows, although astronauts on American missions may not take their own cameras. All the cameras belong to NASA and these will also be used for scientific observations.

THE 24-HOUR DAY

A space station is a closed environment – astronauts can't leave if they decide they'd like to do something else! Imagine your classroom is a space station. The crew of astronauts is you and your classmates. The commander is your teacher.

Your task is find out how much time the astronauts spend on various activities. Over one 24-hour period, note how much time you spend on:

- **scientific activity** *(lessons, homework)*

- **exercise** *(playing football, cycling to school, walking the dog, etc)*

- **leisure pursuits** *(reading, watching TV, playing computer games, etc)*

- **eating** *(include snacks)*

- **maintenance** *(washing, cleaning teeth, getting dressed, tidying your room, etc)*

- **sleeping.**

How much time did the other astronauts in your crew spend on these activities over 24 hours? Can you make a bar chart for each astronaut, showing their scores?

A COOKING CONUNDRUM

Astronauts Caesar, King, Mikado, and Pharaoh are working on the space station. On the menu for dinner are soup, pizza, hamburgers, peas, chips and icecream.

• Each astronaut chooses three things to eat. Each item of food is chosen by two astronauts.

• Two things chosen by Pharaoh are also chosen by King.

• Mikado and Pharaoh both take chips.

• Both the astronauts who have pizza also choose hamburger.

If Mikado picks soup, and King doesn't eat icecream, which two astronauts choose peas?

(You will find the answer on page 30.)

FOOD & DRINK

All the food and water that astronauts use on a space station must be flown up to them. For astronauts on a long tour of several months in space, the arrival of a supply craft is an exciting event. Fresh food is always welcome. In free fall, it is important that food and drink does not spill. Crumbs and splashes that in Earth's gravity would fall to the ground remain hanging in the air, and are difficult to round up. If they get into equipment or experiments, they could do a great deal of damage. For that reason, food and drink are kept in special containers. There is a kitchen, or galley, with a fridge and stove, where food is kept and prepared. The meals are designed to give an astronaut about 2,700 calories a day, and they contain extra calcium and vitamins to help keep the astronauts healthy.

MUSHY MEALS

The first cosmonauts and astronauts were given food in aluminium containers like toothpaste tubes. The food was made into a soft paste, which could be sucked out. Later, when spaceships grew bigger and could carry water, food was freeze-dried and packed in plastic. A special water gun was used to rehydrate it. There was a choice of food and an astronaut could go for four days without eating the same thing.

A TABLE TO EAT AT

The *ISS* has a wardroom, or dining room, where astronauts can eat at a table. Eating together is a good way of relaxing and getting to know each other – important when crews come from many different countries. Dutch and French astronauts like a real break for a good meal. They find the Americans' more casual approach to eating very odd. English is the official language of the space station, but mealtimes may be an opportunity for people with a different native tongue to speak their own languages together.

SNAP UP A SWEETIE

These sweets are as weightless in space as the astronauts. They must be snapped up fast before they become a hazard.

FRESH WATER

Water is one of the most important items supplied to a space station. Fresh water for drinking and cooking is brought in large bags. With a limited amount of space, it is important to use it efficiently. Water on space stations is recycled. On *Mir*, 1 litre of water could be condensed from the air each day for every person aboard. This recycled water is used for things like washing and preparing food.

ORBITING GRAPEFRUIT

At the start of missions, or when a supply craft has arrived, astronauts and cosmonauts can enjoy fresh food. Fruit is always popular. When the fresh food has been eaten, crews have to use dried or canned food.

EAT OFF YOUR LEG

On the shuttle, food restraints make eating easier. To eat, astronauts put their food on a tray, which they strap to their leg. A plastic surround holds the food in place. Knives, forks and spoons can be tied on.

TODAY'S MENU

This carton contains pasta. Modern astronauts can choose from a wide variety of food and drink. On the shuttle, there are over 70 different kinds of food on the menu, and 20 different drinks. There are snacks for anyone who feels hungry between meals. Food can be stored in a fridge, or heated in an oven.

13

DID YOU KNOW?

• *The first parts of the International Space Station were launched in 1998. These were Zarya, the functional cargo block, and Unity, the connecting module. More parts will be added until building is completed in 2004.*

• *When it is completed, the ISS will measure 108.5 metres (355 ft) across and 88.4 metres (300 ft) long. It will be 43.6 metres (143 ft) tall, and weigh more than 453,600 kilos (1,000,006.5 lb).*

• *Once it is built, the ISS will be the third brightest object in the night sky. Only the Moon and Venus will be brighter.*

• *The length of the habitable modules in the ISS will be 79.9 metres (262 ft) — much larger than Salyut at 28 metres (92 ft), Skylab at 26.2 metres (86 ft) and Mir at 29.2 metres (96 feet).*

• *The ISS will fly above 95% of the world's population.*

① DOCKING MODULE

Docking modules are the points where transport vehicles, such as the space shuttle, can be docked, or attached, to the *ISS*. Only when a vehicle has docked can astronauts, equipment or supplies move from one craft to the other (see page 6).

② ZARYA

In 1998, *Zarya* was launched. It was the first module for the *ISS* to go into space (see page 5).

③ SERVICE MODULE

Service modules contain the equipment needed to supply air, power and water to the *ISS*.

④ UNITY

In 1999, *Unity*, the second module for the *ISS*, was joined with *Zarya* (see page 5).

● CUPOLA

The cupola (not visible in main picture) is a ring of windows for observation. From the station, 85% of the globe can be seen.

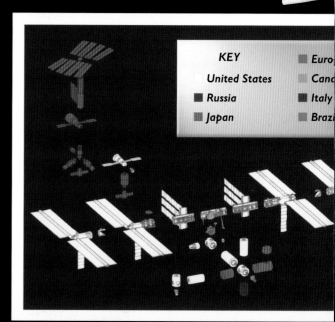

⑤ AIRLOCK

An airlock is where the air pressure between two places, such as the *ISS* and a transport vehicle, can be made equal. Every docking module has an airlock (see page 7).

⑥ DESTINY

The US owns *Destiny*, one of the *ISS*'s six laboratories. It will be used for a wide variety of research, including material, medical and microgravity sciences.

⑦ JAPANESE EXPERIMENT MODULE

This module is made up of four parts; a laboratory, the Experiment Logistics Module, an Exposed Facility (platform) and a Remote Manipulator System (see page 18).

KEY	
	■ Europ
United States	Cana
■ Russia	■ Italy
■ Japan	■ Brazi

THE INTERNATIONAL SPACE STATION

What will the *International Space Station* look like when it is complete? The model shown below gives an idea of the finished construction. It identifies some of the different parts of the space station and explains their function. You can refer to the other pages in this book to find out more about the *ISS* and what life is like for the astronauts who live and work in space.

8 *COLUMBUS*

This is the European Space Agency's laboratory where research is carried out relating to life in space and on Earth (see page 16).

9 *SOLAR ARRAYS*

Some 2,508 sq metres (27,000 sq ft) of solar arrays will provide electricity for the *ISS* using sunlight. They can be turned so that they always face the Sun.

INTERNATIONAL SPACE STATION

Sixteen countries, led by the USA, have joined together to build the *International Space Station*. Using American, Russian, Japanese and European Space Agency rockets, 45 launches will be needed to build the *ISS*. This colour-coded diagram shows which country is contributing each component, but these plans may change before the space station is completed.

10 *TRUSS*

The truss is an aluminium frame. Various parts of the *ISS* are attached to it, including radiator panels, the RMS, radio antennae, and a portable working platform for astronauts. Small carts will carry astronauts and equipment along rails to different parts of the structure. Large solar arrays are attached to each end.

HABITATION MODULE

The habitation module (not visible in main picture) is where astronauts will live on the *ISS*. When completed, the module will join onto the ESA's *Columbus*. The first crew of astronauts – two Russian and one American – will man the station from January 2000.

11 *NODES*

Nodes are large joints that connect the modules of the *ISS* together. Until the habitation module is ready, astronauts will live in nodes and service modules. When the habitation module is in place, nodes will be used for storage.

WORKING INSIDE

A large part of the scientific work on the *International Space Station* is done inside. Each of the six laboratories is equipped for a wide range of experiments. Larger crews of astronauts can work on the *ISS*, making it possible to carry out experiments round the clock. Astronauts will be able to work with scientists back on Earth, using video and computer links, in a way that couldn't be done on earlier, smaller space stations. To activate the station's equipment, scientists will be issued with personal laptop computers which they can plug in wherever they work. Delicate work takes place at special benches, where a gentle draught of air blown downwards by fans will hold small tools and parts steady. The commander and flight engineer will look after the *ISS*, leaving the scientists to do their research.

SPROUTING SEEDS

Scientists have been trying to grow plants in space for many years. They want to find out how the lack of gravity affects seeds. On a long journey in space, plants could provide food and oxygen. To do this, plants would have to grow, flower and seed in space, and the seed itself would have to grow when it was planted in turn. Cosmonauts have grown vegetables like radishes, lettuce and turnips successfully, but other experiments have produced plants with no seeds in the seedheads.

SOCKS IN SPACE

There is no need for people to wear shoes in space. However, astronauts and cosmonauts find their feet get very cold, because the distribution of blood is changed by the lack of gravity. Wearing thick socks is essential.

COLUMBUS

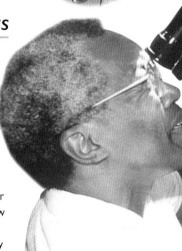

Columbus is the ESA's laboratory on the *ISS*. Scientists working in it will investigate such things as the behaviour of flames, fluids and metals in space. They could discover how to make even better computer chips. Work on tissues and crystals may lead to new treatments for diseases such as cancer and diabetes. Studying the effects of living in free fall on the human body will be very important for future journeys exploring the solar system.

GLOVE BOX EXPERIMENT

Some experiments, especially those using liquids, have to be sealed into special glove boxes. Scientists put their hands in the gloves to reach the experiments. Some of the liquids used could burn skin, eyes or ears if they escaped.

MICROGRAVITY EXPERIMENTS

In space, life sciences and the science of different sorts of materials are studied in microgravity. Many of the results enable new or better products to be manufactured for us to use on Earth.

ORBITING LABORATORIES

The six *ISS* laboratories together give more than four times the laboratory space available on *Mir*. They come from 11 of the 14 countries that make up the ESA, together with Japan, Russia and the USA.

PHOTOGRAPHIC RECORDS

From space, it is possible to study the environment on Earth for long stretches of time. Volcanoes, mountains, forests, oceans and weather patterns can be seen. Pollution caused by humans, such as smog, the destruction of forests, and oil spills at sea, can be observed and photographed. Shannon Lucid and her fellow cosmonauts on *Mir* reported seeing huge clouds of smoke in Mongolia. It was several days before news of enormous forest fires came from people on the ground.

✿ INTERNATIONAL SPACE STATION
WORKING TIMETABLE

30 days	free fall for experiments
10 days	maintenance
30 days	free fall
20 days	general tasks
A crew of six will serve a tour of duty lasting three or six months	

17

EMUS IN SPACE

The Extravehicular Mobility Unit (EMU) is a life-support system fixed to the back of the spacesuit. It weighs 68 kg (150 lb). In the EMU are batteries, oxygen, an air treatment system, and a cooling system. An EMU allows an astronaut to work in space for up to eight hours. SAFER (Simplified Aid for EVA Rescue) is a small rocket attachment, fixed to an EMU. It is used to move an astronaut around. All *ISS* astronauts will use SAFER for working outside.

Under the suit the astronaut wears a second body cover, a web of tiny tubes, filled with water. This keeps an astronaut's body temperature at a comfortable level.

The spacesuits worn on the shuttle weigh about 47 kg (104 lb). The suits, made in three sizes, have a fibreglass shell covering the upper body, and 11 layers of nylon, dacron and kevlar fabric.

The helmet weighs another 4 kg (9 lb). It is fixed to the suit, and the astronaut can turn his head inside. When the suit is filled with air, it becomes very stiff.

WALKING ON THE SHUTTLE

A great deal of work in space is done from the shuttle's cargo bay, seen here looking towards the tail as the shuttle flies over Shark Bay in Australia. Parts for the *ISS* will be carried in the cargo bay. Astronauts will lift them out and fix them in place. This may involve using the Remote Manipulator System (RMS), a robot arm worked from inside the system.

SIX DEGREES OF FREEDOM

The Japanese Experiment Module includes a laboratory, the Experiment Logistics Module (a store for experiments and tools) and an Exposed Facility, or 'back porch' (see pages 14-15). This is a platform in space. Experiments that need to be exposed to microgravity and high vacuum will be placed on the Exposed Facility. Japan is also building two remote manipulator arms. The larger arm will be used to put experiments on the Exposed Facility, and to collect them. The small arm will be used for very precise work. It has six degrees of freedom; it can move up, down, left, right, forward and back, like a human arm.

THE VITAL SPACESUIT

To work outside in space, an astronaut must wear a spacesuit. Space is airless and bitterly cold. Dangerous radiation can kill. A spacesuit protects the wearer from these lethal conditions. Life-support and communication systems are built in. The suit is only worn for Extravehicular Activity (EVA). A different spacesuit is worn for launching and landing.

WORKING OUTSIDE

One of the first jobs that *International Space Station* astronauts will do in space is to build the space station itself! It will take about 850 hours of spacewalks, spread over five years, to put the different parts of the station together. Those modules already in space must also be maintained. Canada is building a robot manipulator arm, 16.8 metres (55 ft) long, which will be used for building and servicing work. It can handle payloads that weigh up to 125 tonnes on Earth. Some scientific work will be done outside. Space itself will be studied. Scientists want to know more about how the Universe developed, and what gravity is. Their research will also include studying atoms that have been cooled to nearly absolute zero, the lowest possible temperature (-273.15°C/ -459.67°F). It will be possible to find out what effect radiation dust, and other conditions in space have on materials. This is important for designing and building long-distance spacecraft in the future.

SPACE ACTIVITY

LIGHT PRINTS

Visible light is a form of electromagnetic radiation. In daytime, we can see when visible light from the Sun reaches us.

Light can do other things! Try printing with light – you must wait for a very sunny day to do this, though.

YOU WILL NEED:

paper
bright red or blue paint
small, solid objects, such as a spoon, a cotton reel, a leaf, a key, a button

WHAT YOU DO:

• Cover one side of a sheet of paper with a thick layer of paint. Leave it to dry.

• Put the paper outside in full sunlight, and arrange the objects on top of it.

• Leave the paper in sunlight for several hours, then remove the objects. What has happened?

Try the same experiment on a bright but overcast day. Leave the objects on the painted paper outside for twice as long. What happens?

THE FLYING ARMCHAIR

The Manned Manoeuvring Unit (MMU) lets a shuttle astronaut move about in space. It is a backpack shaped like an armchair, powered by 24 small thrusters. These are worked by push-button and joystick controls on the armrests. Sitting in an MMU, an astronaut can move in any direction and even turn somersaults.

THE GOLDEN SLIPPERS

When astronauts work outside using the Remote Manipulator System (RMS), their feet are clamped to it with foot restraints nicknamed the Golden Slippers. The RMS on the shuttle was built by Canada. The arm has three joints, shoulder, elbow and wrist. Two television cameras are mounted on it so that its movements can be watched from inside the shuttle.

GOING HOME

Astronauts about to return to Earth must get used to the effects of gravity after being in free fall. If blood suddenly pooled in the lower part of the body, draining away from the brain, it would cause blackouts. The lower body negative pressure device pulls fluids down from where they collect in the upper body, and returns them to the lower part of an astronaut's body. Cosmonauts on *Mir* wear a gravity acclimatization suit to help them get used to gravity again.

EXERCISE TIME

Every astronaut must exercise for at least one hour every day, and this time is built into the schedule. By using a different exercise machine each day, crew members work every part of their bodies in turn. These machines stop muscles wasting away. Pressure belts on the tops of the legs help control the blood flow until the astronaut's body gets used to being in space. Before they return to Earth, astronauts must get used to the strains that gravity will put on their bodies. When they exercise in space, the sweat doesn't drip downwards. It turns into puddles that fly about. Astronauts have to towel up their sweat, or it will drift about and become a nuisance.

SPACE
ACTIVITY

BODYCHECK

Astronauts check their bodies regularly, to see how they are affected by living and working in space. Run some checks on your body to see how it works at different times.

• For a week, take your temperature as soon as you get up in the morning and again just before you go to bed. Write down the results. What do you notice?

• When you have been running, or playing an energetic game, take your temperature again. Write down the result. Has your temperature changed?

• Doctors measure your pulse to see how often your heart beats. The easiest pulse to find is in your wrist, just below your thumb. Find it in one wrist using the thumb of your other hand.

• Watch your pulse at work! Push a drawing pin into the end of a matchstick. Lay your wrist on a solid surface and carefully balance the drawing pin on your pulse. Can you count the beats?

What happens to your pulse when you've been running?

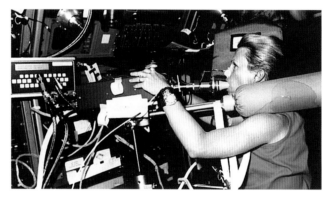

GETTING USED TO SPACE

During their first few days in space, astronauts feel light-headed and their faces go puffy. This is connected with their blood collecting in their chests. Their brains think there is a lot of extra liquid in their bodies and the astronauts often need to go to the lavatory. Astronauts must drink plenty of water to stop their bodies getting too dry.

SPACE SICKNESS

The third man in space, Soviet cosmonaut Gherman Titov, was the first to report feeling sick in orbit. Since then, many astronauts have suffered from space sickness. It is caused because the brain gets confusing messages from the eyes and the balancing mechanisms found in the inner ear. Astronauts generally recover quickly, but it helps if they don't move their heads suddenly, don't do any acrobatics in free fall, and keep away from disorientating views that might make them feel giddy. After a while, their bodies get used to being in space.

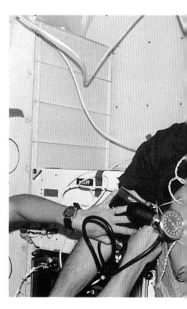

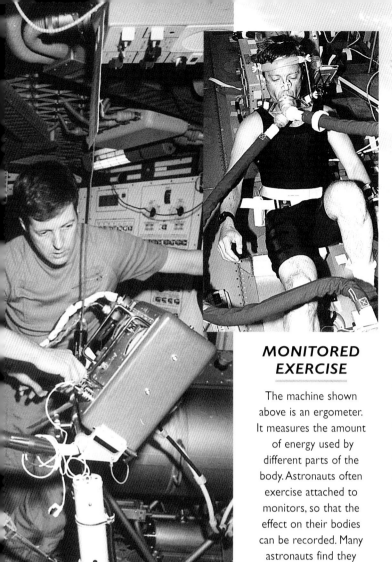

HEALTH

Soviet cosmonaut Yuri Gagarin was the first man to go into space. When he made a single orbit of Earth in 1961, no one knew if a man could survive in space. Gagarin came back safely, but scientists still didn't know what would happen to the human body if it stayed in space for a long time. Since then, they have been gathering information. Astronauts, including several doctors, have tested themselves and each other. Paying attention to health is important in space. Without exercise, muscles waste away, and bones lose their density. Blood, which on Earth is pulled downwards by gravity, pools higher up the body, in the chest. The workings of the heart change. Some astronauts suffer from space sickness. Space stations have a medical kit as part of their equipment. This contains enough medicines to cure astronauts of stomach upsets and minor infections. The drugs are prescribed by the flight surgeon, who may be a doctor or a crew member trained in first aid. So far, there has been no need to carry out an operation in space.

MONITORED EXERCISE

The machine shown above is an ergometer. It measures the amount of energy used by different parts of the body. Astronauts often exercise attached to monitors, so that the effect on their bodies can be recorded. Many astronauts find they have lost weight when they get back to Earth. Even so, the muscles on their arms and shoulders become very strong, because they are used frequently to move cargo around.

LEARNING BY HEART

On Earth, a heart beats about 70 times a minute during sleep. In space, it slows down to about 30 beats a minute. Microgravity puts great stress on the heart. It changes the heart's position, moving it up inside the chest. Astronauts check their blood pressure frequently. This picture shows Senator Jake Garn, who was chairman of the budget committee that decided how much money NASA could have. He flew on *Discovery* in 1985, and was tested along with the other astronauts.

DOCTORS IN SPACE

American astronaut Kay Hire was one of a crew of doctors who worked on *Spacelab* in 1998. For this mission, the space station was renamed *Neurolab*. It was full of experiments to test the body's nervous system, including balance, sleep patterns and co-ordination. On Earth, these can be affected by many illnesses. The doctors measured their blood pressure and the way blood flowed into their brains. This gave them useful information on how blood moves round our bodies when it does not have to work against gravity.

DAILY ROUTINE

To do all the work on the space station, the station itself must work properly. Each crew of astronauts on the *ISS* has a commander and a flight engineer. They look after the station, leaving the scientists free to concentrate on their work. Gravity pulls everything in low-Earth orbit down. To stay at the right height, spacecraft need to fire booster rockets at regular intervals. The *ISS* timetable allows reboosting every 90 days. In this way it should stay in orbit for at least 15 years. A *Soyuz* spacecraft will be attached to the space station as an Assured Crew Return Vehicle – or 'lifeboat' – and will be changed every six months to ensure that the batteries work!

POWER CUT

In 1997, a supply ferry crashed into four of *Mir's* solar panels. The module *Spektr* was also damaged, and started to lose air. The cosmonauts had to switch off all the electricity to repair the leak. They could not use *Mir's* batteries to turn the solar panels to the Sun to make electricity. Instead, they used the power in their *Soyuz* lifeboat to turn the whole of *Mir* so that the undamaged solar panels faced the Sun.

SPACE ACTIVITY

THE BALLOON THAT DOESN'T GO 'BANG!'

Astronauts working on a space station need air to breathe. It is pumped through the station and kept at a comfortable pressure.

When you blow up a balloon, you squash air into a small space. It is under pressure, pushing hard against the thin rubber skin of the balloon. If it gets the chance, the air will escape as fast as it can. What happens when you stick a needle into a blown-up balloon? It goes bang! Well, not always...

WHAT YOU NEED:

a balloon
sticky tape
a knitting needle

WHAT YOU DO:

• Blow up the balloon, and tie the end so the air can't get out.

• Tear off a strip of sticky tape, and stick it down firmly on one side of the balloon.

• Tear off another strip of tape, and stick it down on the other side of the balloon.

• Poke the knitting needle through one of the tape strips and into the balloon.

• As you push, guide it so it comes out through the second strip of tape.

The balloon hasn't burst! Can you find out why? How long does it take for the balloon to go down?

DAMAGING DEBRIS

A minute speck of paint once hit a shuttle and made a hole 0.5 cm (0.2 in) across on a window. There is a lot of debris in space and it can travel at up to 28,160 km/h (17,500 mph). It includes things such as meteoroids, dust and small pebbles. When these fall into Earth's atmosphere, they burn up, and we see meteors, or shooting stars. There are also pieces of old rockets and satellites in orbit. If any of this debris hit the space station, it could cause serious damage. Every centimetre of the outside structure must be regularly checked.

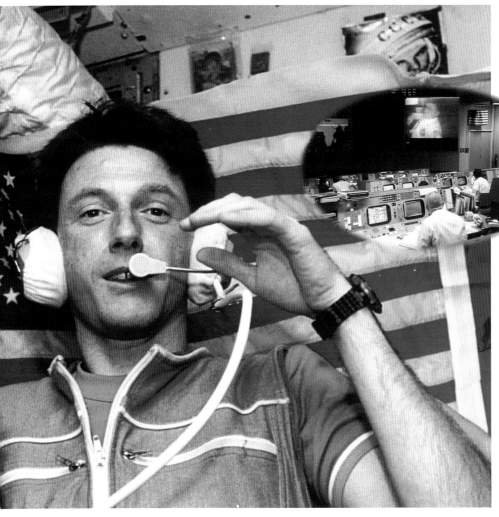

MISSION CONTROL

Mission control is the base on the ground that oversees every part of a space mission. Scientists at mission control are in touch with the *ISS* at all times. They keep track of its position, give instructions and take reports from the astronauts. They also pass messages between astronauts and their families. Radio signals bounced off communications satellites are used. One of the problems faced by the crews on *Mir* was that they couldn't communicate with mission control all the time. It had to be passing over a ground station in Russia to make contact. This happened once in an orbit, about every 90 minutes, enabling the crew to talk for about 10 minutes. A cosmonaut was always on duty 'on comm', in case mission control needed to talk to *Mir*.

SUPPLYING ELECTRICITY

The electricity system on the *ISS* uses nearly 13 km (8 miles) of electric wire. Astronauts need to know how to repair the system if it breaks down. The electricity used to power space stations is made using solar arrays. Each solar array is covered in rows of photovoltaic cells made of silicon. These use the Sun's energy to make electricity which is then stored in batteries.

RUBBISH!

On a space station, there is not much room to store rubbish. Some is returned to Earth for disposal, packed into visiting spacecraft. On *Mir*, unmanned supply craft were filled full of rubbish. When they fell back to Earth, the rubbish burned up in the atmosphere along with the ferries. Astronauts have to squash rubbish so that it takes up as little room as possible. The shuttle has a trash compactor that crushes rubbish (left).

AIR SUPPLY

Keeping air moving through a space station is a big problem. On Earth, convection currents keep air fresh. As there is no convection current on a space station, air has to be moved around using fans and pumps which are kept on all the time. As well as being noisy, they dry out the air and cause draughts. Sometimes the air gets very smelly – for example, if food is being cooked. To take out the carbon dioxide that builds up in stale air, the air is 'scrubbed' before it is recycled.

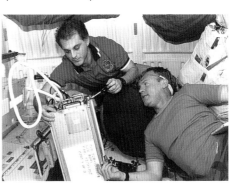

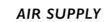

GLIDING TO EARTH

Astronauts coming home in the shuttle glide to Earth. As it falls through the atmosphere, the shuttle gets very hot. A coat of ceramic tiles protects the crew inside from temperatures of up to 1,260°C (2,300°F). The air around the shuttle glows, and the heat is so fierce that radio contact is lost for about 10 minutes. A parachute helps to brake the shuttle as it touches the ground.

G-FORCES

On the journey back to Earth, for a short time the astronaut's body has to stand up to a load of three or four gravities. This is much easier to do if the astronauts lie flat on bunks, with their feet above their heads.

THE LAST SOVIET CITIZEN

An astronaut or cosmonaut may have spent months looking at Earth from space. Dr Valeri Polyakov stayed on *Mir* for 437 days and 18 hours (from 8 January 1994 to 22 March 1995), setting a world record. When Sergei Krikalev got back to Earth in 1992, the old Soviet Union which he had left 312 days earlier had disappeared. There had been dramatic political changes. The country had taken back its old name, Russia. Krikalev (who is listed as the flight engineer for the first crew on the *ISS*) was nicknamed 'the last Soviet citizen'.

A HEROES' WELCOME

The first people to travel in space returned to Earth as heroes. The city of New York gave the crew of *Apollo 11*, the first men to walk on the Moon, a traditional ticker tape welcome. It was one of the biggest parades in the city's history. Standing in the open car are Neil Armstrong, Michael Collins, and Edwin 'Buzz' Aldrin.

GOING HOME

At the end of each tour of duty on the space station, the astronauts returning to Earth hand over experiments in progress to the new crews. Results of experiments, notes and other materials are carefully packed to withstand the journey home. Towards the end of long missions, astronauts take extra calcium and vitamins to help them recover from the effects of being in space. Back on Earth, astronauts often find their leg muscles are weak, even after plenty of exercise, but swimming helps to restore them. Having floated about in space, many astronauts forget they can't do this back on Earth. They may try to float out of bed, or put things down in the air, so they need time to adjust. When they reach Earth, the astronauts are debriefed. Doctors check them to make sure they are healthy after their time in space.

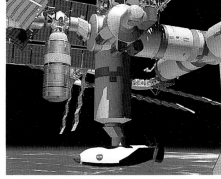

HOMEWARD BOUND

The transporter vehicle that is to bring a crew of astronauts back to Earth docks with the space station, using one of the docking ports. Then the airlock is activated, so that the air pressure and oxygen levels can be made equal, just as when astronauts arrive at the station. New crew members and supplies leave the transporter for the space station, then the astronauts returning to Earth board for their journey home.

25

CITIES IN THE SKY

Humans have travelled in space for less than 40 years. In that time, our ability to do things in space has improved enormously. Scientists hope that soon a base in which people can live and work will be built on the Moon. If this happens, a space station will be needed as a half-way point. Here, people and supplies would be collected and ferried backwards and forwards to the Moon. Space scientists want to use the *ISS* as such a base. It could be used to send an astronaut to Mars, and perhaps also to journey to other parts of the solar system. Living on the Moon, or possibly on other planets, will allow scientists to find out more about the Universe and how it works. Useful minerals may be mined. It may be possible to build cities in space, capable of growing enough food to feed their citizens. In a world that is over-populated and which is running out of food and natural resources, space offers a future full of hope.

SPACE ACTIVITY

A FROSTY CHALLENGE

If there is ice on the Moon, it will be easier to build a base there. Ice behaves in interesting ways, as this experiment shows. Your challenge is to cut an ice cube in two! Ask an adult to help you.

YOU WILL NEED:

about 20 cm (8 in) of thin wire
two pencils
an ice cube
a small glass bottle

WHAT YOU DO:

• Wrap each end of the wire around the middle of the pencils to make two 'handles'.

• Put the ice cube on the top of the bottle.

• Holding the pencil 'handles' push the wire down hard on the ice cube. The wire cuts through the ice cube. But do you have two pieces of ice?

What has happened? Why?

BUILDING SPACECRAFT

To travel farther into space than the Moon, it will be necessary to build spacecraft that have closed life support systems. This means they will have to produce all the food, water, oxygen and energy used on the journey. Such a spacecraft would probably be built at a space station, or at a base on the Moon. It would have to avoid using up fuel to get through Earth's atmosphere when it was launched.

FUELLING SPACECRAFT

The space shuttle uses 680,000 kg of fuel in 8 minutes. A manned spacecraft would need a huge amount of fuel to take it to the farthest part of the solar system, or beyond. One solution to the problem might be to build spacecraft with engines powered by nuclear fusion. Even using this kind of energy, a spacecraft that travelled any distance in space would have to weigh thousands of tonnes, and most of the weight would be fuel. The nearest star to Earth is Alpha Centauri, 4.34 light years away. Using present fuels, it would take many lifetimes to reach it. We cannot yet travel faster than light.

A DESERT OF ROCKS

Astronauts landing on the Moon would be faced with a desert of rocks and dust. The *Lunar Prospector* probe, launched in 1998, found signs that made some scientists think there could be ice at the Moon's poles. If there is ice, water wouldn't have to be carried to the Moon. Instead, it could be obtained by thawing the ice. The oxygen and hydrogen in the water could be used to make an atmosphere to breathe, and fuel for general use.

SELF-SUPPORTING STATIONS

No one has yet been able to design a space station that is completely self-supporting. Even the *ISS* will need regular visits from supply ferries. To travel as far as Mars, astronauts will need foolproof ways of using – and reusing – air, water and food.

LUNAR BASE

There is no atmosphere on the Moon. A lunar base would have to be completely enclosed, so that oxygen could be supplied to people living inside. Airlocks would allow people to go in and out without letting oxygen escape into space. Anyone outside the base would have to wear a space suit. This would allow breathing, and also protect the body from the fierce temperatures, ranging from 127°C (260°F) to -173°C (-280°F).

MOON SHUTTLE

A launch pad for spacecraft would be placed at some distance from the base, for safety. Small ferries would fetch and carry people and supplies between the Moon and a large orbiting spacecraft or a space station.

WORKING ON THE MOON

To travel any distance over the surface of the Moon, astronauts would use some kind of roving vehicle. It could be used to explore the Moon, looking for metals and minerals, or for transporting workers to mines, or to structures where plants used for food and making oxygen were grown in hydroponic gardens.

IT CAME FROM SPACE

Space – and space stations – may sometimes seem very remote. Only a few hundred people have been in space. Some people ask whether the billions of dollars it costs to build a space station is money well-spent. But ever since humans first went into space, we have benefitted from technologies developed for the space programme. In space, tools and materials have to withstand bitter cold and must work in a vacuum. Designs that work on Earth because they use the force of gravity are useless in space. Anything used in space must be very strong and light enough for astronauts to carry and use comfortably. All tools must be reliable. Many people are employed by the new industries which have grown up to make goods that use these new technologies. **NASA** has set up an **Office of Technology Transfer and Commercialization.** This now works with private companies to develop products from the research and discoveries **NASA** has initiated. Many space spin-offs have been used in medicine to help sick people, for example a tiny pump that could be implanted in the hearts of people with cardiac diseases.

BODY SCANNER

Body scanners help doctors see what is happening inside a human body. They were developed from a machine that helped NASA make photos of the Moon clearer. The type of machines that monitor astronauts' bodies are now widely used in hospitals.

THE NON-STICK SAUCEPAN

Teflon – scientists know it as polytetrafluoroethene, or PTFE – was developed specially for use in space. The metal surface on the inside of a non-stick saucepan is coated with this material. It is extremely strong and very light. It rarely reacts to chemicals; doesn't change when exposed to great heat and has a very low coefficient of friction – the scientific way of saying that it doesn't stick to anything!

SANDWICH WRAPPERS

Have you ever bought a sandwich packed in a triangular clear plastic box? This kind of wrapping was used to keep food for astronauts fresh in the early days of space travel in the 1960s.

THE SILVERDOME ROOF

Teflon, or PTFE, has been used to build enormous, unsupported roofs, such as the ones on the Silverdome football stadium, home of the Detroit Lions in the USA, and Jedda airport in Saudi Arabia.

SPACE PEN

On Earth, the ink in a pen is pulled down by gravity from a reservoir like a cartridge. As there is no gravity in space, some astronauts use pencils. Pens like the one show here, in which the ink is pushed down to the nib, are also used.

CORDLESS TOOLS

When an astronaut is working in space, there are no handy electric sockets around to plug in tools. Battery-powered tools were the answer. We now take tools like this cordless drill for granted.

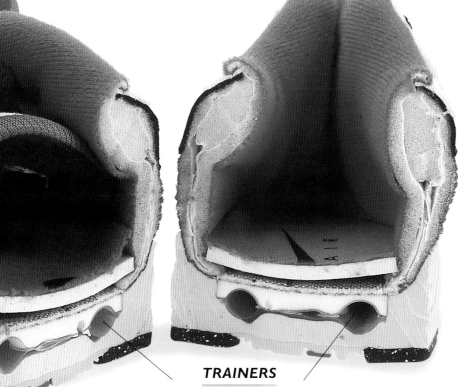

TRAINERS

Shoes used by astronauts training for life in free fall had soles with pockets of air in them. Now many sports shoes have soles like this.

THE DIGITAL WATCH

Astronauts need to keep time very accurately. Digital watches were first produced for them to use.

SMOKE ALARM

Fire is a serious danger in space. Smoke detectors were developed to give astronauts on *Skylab* early warning of fire. A light-sensitive photocell sounds an alarm when smoke dims the light.

GLOSSARY

APOLLO

The Apollo Program was the American project that aimed to put a man on the Moon. There were 17 Apollo missions in all. The first ten were unmanned. Starting in 1969 with *Apollo 11*, there were six successful manned missions to the Moon.

ATMOSPHERIC PRESSURE

Atmospheric pressure measures the weight of the gases in an atmosphere as they press downwards onto the surface of a planet or other heavenly body. On Earth, atmospheric pressure is usually measured from sea level. In a spacecraft, atmospheric pressure is created by compressing oxygen and other gases.

CONVECTION CURRENT

A convection current is a movement of heat. When air gets hot, it expands and moves upwards. As it rises, it cools down and contracts. It takes up less space, and moves downwards.

COSMONAUT

A cosmonaut is the name the Russians give their astronauts.

ESA (EUROPEAN SPACE AGENCY)

The European Space Agency is the body that organizes the space programme for the 14 European countries which are members.

EVA (EXTRA VEHICULAR ACTIVITY)

An EVA, or Extra Vehicular Activity, is spacewalking. EVAs are used for work or any other activity by an astronaut outside a spacecraft.

FREE FALL

Free fall is the correct name for weightlessness. Free fall is caused because Earth still exerts a gravitational pull on a spacecraft in orbit. This is cancelled out by the spacecraft's forward movement.

The craft and everything in it are falling endlessly round Earth. When things fall, they have no weight. Astronauts are taught how to work in free fall.

GRAVITY

Gravity is the attractive force, or gravitational pull, that Earth exerts on objects on its surface or nearby in space. Every heavenly body has a force of gravity. The larger the body, the stronger the gravitational pull. The weight of an object is caused by gravity.

HYDROPONIC GARDEN

A hydroponic garden is a way of growing plants that does not use soil. Instead, water mixed with liquid fertilisers is used. The plants' roots are usually supported by sand or pebbles.

LIGHT YEAR

A light year is a measurement. It is the distance light travels in a year, about 9.46 million million kilometres. Light years are used to measure the distances between Earth and heavenly bodies outside the solar system.

MICROGRAVITY

Microgravity is the state of weightlessness experienced in free fall. In microgravity, conditions that result from gravity, such as convection, do not exist, or are very faint. Microgravity also describes scientific processes that are carried out in a gravity-free environment.

MISSION

A mission is a journey in space made by a spacecraft and the tasks to be performed. Many missions are manned by astronauts.

MODULE

A module is a self-contained unit of a spacecraft.

NASA

The National Aeronautics and Space Administration, or NASA, is the body which organizes the US space programme.

ORBIT

An orbit is the path taken in space by one body as it travels round another body. An orbiting body can be natural or man-made. Most orbits are elliptical in shape.

PAYLOAD

A payload is the cargo on a space shuttle. It includes all the equipment in the payload bay, such as a satellite, or experiments, and any equipment a crew member takes on board that is not part of the shuttle's usual flight equipment.

PHOTOVOLTAIC CELLS

A photovoltaic cell is made of two layers of the mineral silicon. When light from the Sun falls on the silicon, electrons are released, making an electric current. This current is stored in batteries until it is needed. Many rows of photovoltaic cells form solar arrays.

RADIATION

Radiation, or electromagnetic radiation, is a kind of energy found everywhere in the universe. It moves in waves of different lengths. Radio waves are the longest. Microwaves, infra-red, visible light, ultraviolet, X-rays and gamma rays are all forms of electromagnetic radiation. Some forms of radiation are deadly. Earth is protected from them by its atmosphere.

REHYDRATION

Rehydration is the process of adding water to a substance which has been dried to bring it back to its normal state. Dried

food, which is light, keeps well and is easy to pack, is rehydrated before it is eaten.

SATELLITE

A satellite is a small body in orbit round a larger body in space. A satellite can be natural, like the Moon, or man-made, like a space station.

SOLAR ARRAY

A solar array is a bank of cells that make electricity using sunlight. The cells are arranged on a panel that sticks out from a spacecraft. Solar arrays are often called solar panels.

SOLAR SYSTEM

The solar system is the Sun and all the heavenly bodies that orbit the Sun. It includes the planets, moons, comets, dust and gas.

SOVIET UNION (USSR)

The Soviet Union was a political grouping of 15 countries in Eastern Europe and Asia. The most powerful member was Russia. The Soviet Union came to an end in 1991.

SPACE SHUTTLE

The space shuttle is the popular name for the STS, or Space Transportation System. It is a piloted spacecraft that can be reused. The space shuttle is launched into space using rockets, and returns to Earth as a glider. There are four space shuttles.

WEIGHTLESSNESS

Weightlessness is the absence of the effects of gravity. It is a state experienced in orbit in which objects seem to have no weight. The correct name for weighlessness is free fall.

SPACE ACTIVITIES ANSWERS

SLEEPING SCIENTISTS

COOKING CONUNDRUM

Astronauts Caesar and King chose peas. You can work it out with a table, like this:

	soup	pizza	hamburger	peas	chips	icecream
Caesar	x			x		x
King		x	x	x		
Mikado	x				x	x
Pharaoh		x	x		x	

WEBSITE ADDRESSES

You can find out a lot more about space and the *ISS* on the Internet. Why not visit these websites:

NASA http://station.nasa.gov/station/index.html
http://station.nasa.gov/gallery/video/station/mmats/index.html
http://spaceflight.nasa.gov/index.html

NASDA http://spaceboy.nasda.go.jp/qanda/qanda
_e/qastronaut_e.html

ESA http://www.estec.esa.nl/spaceflight

ESTEC http://www.estec.esa.nl/

MACMILLAN CHILDREN'S BOOKS

GIRAFFE ON A
BICYCLE

Julia Woolf

Monkey found a bicycle.

Luckily, giraffe knew
how to ride it . . .

. . . sort of!

ding!

First they wiggled
one way.

Then they wobbled
the other.

But practice
makes perfect . . .

... and off they went!

ding!
ding!

High in the branches,
a stripy tiger was
enjoying a snooze.
But not for long!

"Wakey, wakey, sleepyhead!" shouted monkey. "Join us for some fun!"

So tiger did.

And off they went, bumpety bump.

As they pedalled through the trees, three leaping lemurs popped out of the leaves.

"The more, the merrier!" monkey cried.
"Who else will join our jungle ride?"

ding!
ding!

A slithering snake was considering a snack when . . .

"Only us!" monkey chattered.
"Plenty of room for you!"

And before long, a surprised
crocodile found he was
a passenger too.

"Up you come," giggled monkey. "Make it snappy!"

Down at the lagoon,
a friendly flamingo
wanted to play.

With a flip and a flap, she joined the fun.

As they sped through the vines, three cheeky monkeys dropped from the skies.

Faster! Faster!

ding!

ding!   DING!

DING!

Whooshing through the jungle
was so much fun until . . .

"LOOK OUT!"

shouted monkey.

CRASH!

And up, up, up they went.

"OH NO!"

shouted everybody.

The animals had broken the bicycle!

But luckily they knew just how to fix it.

First snake snatched the saddle.

Then giraffe grabbed the basket.

Everyone knew what to do.

And soon the bike
was as good as new . . .

. . . sort of.
And home they went.

ding!